ALL GRANADA

6th Edition, April 1984

I.S.B.N.

Spanish	84-378-0492-2
French	84-378-0494-9
English	84-378-0495-7
German	84-378-0496-5
Italian	84-378-0493-0

Dep. Legal B. 11751-1984

 **escudo de oro, s.a.** Palaudarias, 26 - Barcelona, 4 - Spain

Impreso en España - Printed in Spain
F.I.S.A. Palaudarias, 26 - Barcelona-4

In this XVI century engraving, made when Moslem rule was still recent, one can see the architectural features which were, and still largely are, the main points of the town and countryside of Granada. Above and in the centre the impressive outlines of the Alhambra; on the right the city dominating the beautiful and fertile plain; and on the left the wonderful situation of the Generalife. This delightful print, which can be seen in the Casa de los Tiros, is remarkable for the manner in which it illustrates the history of Granada.

FROM TURDULAN ILIVERIR TO MOSLEM GRANADA

It appears that the lands of Granada had contact with people of an advanced civilisation from prehistoric times.

The earliest historical records however relate to the Turdulos who were one of the most civilised of the Iberian tribes and eventually minted coins on which Granada appears under the name of *Iliverir*. Later came the Phoenicians, Greeks and Carthaginians. The latter established themselves nearby in an important aboriginal settlement, and this has recently been confirmed by the discovery of an Iberian sculpture, the Dama de Baza, in the province of Granada.

The arrival of the Romans in the fertile plains around Granada marked an important period in history, and a Roman Town — later to become the city of the Alhambra — was established. It was there that Saint Cecilio founded an Episcopal See in the year 62, and a little more than two centuries later the first Catholic Council in the whole of the Iberian Peninsula was set up.

Ancient *Iliberis* — the Roman name for *Iliverir* — grew in importance under the Visigothic Monarchy and reached its highest point with the arrival of the Arabs.

A view of Granada, with the walls in the foreground and the Alhambra in the centre.

"The Surrender of Granada", the famous picture by Pradilla.

A study of the old Alcazaba of Granada.

THE ARABS AND THE ALHAMBRA

About the middle of the VII Century the Arabs, already well established in the area of Granada, made the town of Castilia the capital city and changed its name to Medina Elvira. It remained the capital of Granada from the time of Omeya Abderramán until that of Zawí ben Zirí. But when the Caliphate of Córdoba was in decline — corroded by internal struggles — Zawí ben Zirí, a valiant viceroy of the Omeyas, created a kingdom out of those lands of Granada which lay at the foot of the Sierra Nevada. Shortly afterwards, in the year 1013, the capital was moved to the site of the present city of Granada, and thus began during this reign a long period of history — not without splendour — which was ended by the Catholic Monarchs on the 2nd of January 1492. Granada grew and developed in splendour under the rule of the Almorávides — who took over from the Ziris in the XI Century — and also under the Almohades. The result of these many years of Arab rule was that their influence penetrated into every corner of the city. The most glorious period of Mohammedan Granada began about the year 1236 when, on the fall of Córdoba to the Christians, it became the capital in fact and by right of Moslem Spain. And it was precisely during this splendid period in Granada's history that the Arab's refined genius created the architectural marvel of the Alhambra.

The Alhambra looks out over the countryside with indolent Moorish majesty.

The graceful outline of the Alhambra
and the restrained Renaissance
architecture of the Palace of Carlos V
stand amid the green countryside,
forming part of its picture and
completing it.

The unmistakable outline of the Alhambra rises on a hill on the left bank of the river Darro. It is opposite the site of the ancient Iliberia which today is occupied by the districts of Albaicín and the Alcazaba. It is a strategic point from which one gets a wide view over the valleys of the Darro to the north and of the Assabica to the south, and to the east can be seen the Albaicín, Mount Mauror and the Cerro del Sol, crowned by the Generalife.

The Alhambra is surrounded by walls within which took place not a few of the bloody battles which form part of the history of the kingdom of Granada. According to Arab chroniclers the name Alhambra is derived from the fact that the ancient fortress was rebuilt at night by the reddish glow of flickering torches. It seems however that the origin of the name comes rather from the colour given to its walls by the ferruginous soil on which the Alhambra is built. In accordance with this theory the name of *Alhambra* comes from the combination of the Spanish version of two Arab words *Calat-alhamrá*, meaning the red castle.

The unmistakable Alhambra stands out against the deep blue of the night sky.

The harmonious architecture of the horse-shoe shaped arch of the Puerta de la Justicia scarcely gives a hint of the marvellous world which lies beyond.

The Puerta del Vino, which leads to the Plaza de los Aljibes, still retains all its medieval elegance.

A fine night scene of the Puerta del Vino and the towers of the Alcazaba.

The Alcazaba was partly rebuilt by Savvar ben Hamdum in the year 889, and over the years it was repeatedly enlarged. By the XI Century, when the Kings of the Zirí dynasty took up residence on the hill of the Albaicín, a wall was built round the Castle of the Alhambra which then became the most important fortress in Granada. Two centuries later, Mohammed ben Alahmar joined the palace and the fortress, and thus began for the Alhambra its most splendid period.

If you climb the hill to the Alhambra by way of the Cuesta de Gomérez, starting at the Plaza Nueva in the very centre of the town, you will see some magnificent views over the forest which extends from the Puerta de las Granadas as far as the Palacio de Carlos V beside the Gate of Justice, which was originally in Arab times the main entrance to this fantastic city of the Kings of Granada.

The beautiful horse-shoe arch of the Puerta de la Justicia stands as an artistic foretaste of the wonderful architecture of the Alhambra which lies beyond. Within the entrance is a small archway, which is also horse-shoe

shaped and curves gracefully over a small doorway of white marble. All the inside walls are decorated with valuable glazed tiles in relief. Even the least impressionable viewer cannot help being dazzled when he sees this marvellous beauty.

In a recess in one of the walls there is a statue of the Virgin with the Child in her arms. Beyond the Puerta de la Justicia is a world that today is only a memory—but a memory that lives on in the beauty of this monument to exquisite art.

Leaving behind the Puerta de la Justicia one arrives at the Plaza de los Aljibes where stands the Puerta del Vino surrounded by many graceful fountains and poetic gardens. Gradually the unique enchantment of the Alhambra begins to take effect and is emphasized by the inscription carved over the gateway—"God alone is the conqueror".

From the Plaza de los Aljibes, leaving to one side the Alcazaba and immediately opposite the Palacio de Carlos V, one enters the Moorish palace and now one is already right inside the Alhambra.

An original view of the Albaicín, seen from one of the magnificent belvederes of the Alhambra.

The Patio of the Arrayanes, a wonder of poetic beauty.

However, in the Plaza de los Aljibes you will have already seen, from a magnificent look-out point over the city, a dramatic panorama that will for ever remain engraved on your memory. The most outstanding features are: the valley of the Darro, the Albaicín, the Sacromonte, the plain and, beyond, the outlines of the Sierra Nevada and the Sierra Elvira and the adjoining ranges of jagged mountains.

In the words of the eminent Arabist García Gómez —"The Alhambra is not only the most beautiful but also the best preserved and most ancient of all the old Moorish palaces remaining in the world." Once inside the Royal Alcázar one has the impression of a setting worthy of "The One Thousand and One Nights". Whether it be the Mexuar (the Cuarto Dorado), the Serrallo (the Cuarto de Comares), or the Harem (the Cuarto de los Leones), there is always that same exquisite and perfumed athosphere. It is something intangible and ethereal which emanates evocatively from these sumptious halls consecrated by the grace of Mohammedan art.

The Mexuar was the place where the Kings of Granada received their subjects in audience. Here it

A view of the Patio de los Arrayanes, taken from the high gallery.

The magnificently worked entrance door to the Sala de la Barca.

A corner of the Patio of the Arrayanes where one can marvel at the filigree work of the slender arches towering above the tiny fountain.

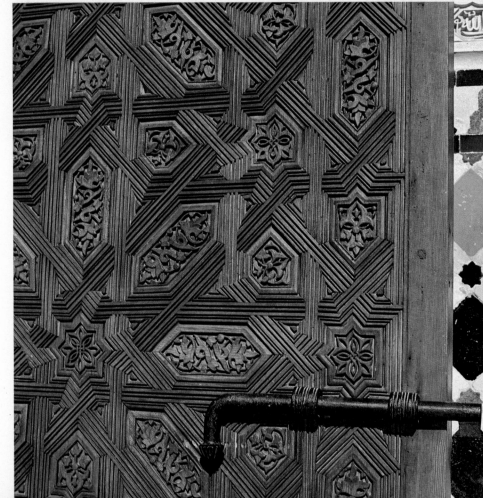

The Albaicín and the Torre del Homenaje, seen from the Sala de Embajadores in the Torre de Comares.

was that all government and legal matters were discussed, but the magic of the Alhambra overcomes the realities of the past and today gives rise only to an atmosphere of peace.

Under the unique spell of the Alhambra one has already crossed the boundary between the dream world and reality, and entering further into the interior one arrives by way of the Patio del Mexuar at the ancient residence of the Arab Kings, the Serrallo or the Cuarto de Comares. This is without doubt a palace of incomparable beauty and one of the most interesting and luxurious places in the Alhambra. The delicate complexity of its decoration and ornamental richness is overwhelming an one's mind becomes intoxicated by the rapture of seeing such splendour. The polichromed tyles and filigreed plaster work create a world of pure fantasy.

If you enter the door to the left you come to the Patio de los Arrayanes. Here the air, the light, the water and the foliage combine in joyful harmony with the architectural design, and make this patio typical of the Alhambra in the way that everything is subjugated to the pleasure of living and every

*The decoration of the Patio del Mexuar
might well be an illustration for a scene
from "A Thousand and One Nights".*

Gazing at the cool elegance of the Sala del Mexuar you get the strange sensation that the past is magically coming to life.

part is designed to give the maximum delight to the senses. Without doubt there are certain places which are particularly delightful and satisfying in every way—full of grace and artistic harmony—and the Patio de los Arrayanes is certainly one of these.

This patio is considered to be a model of the typical patios of Granada. Its grace, the architectural balance and the intelligent use made of natural elements combine in making a memorable picture of harmonious beauty. The disposition of the arches, apart from their filigreed decoration, remind one strongly of Greek architecture.

The roof of the gallery, which is made of wood and was partially destroyed by fire in 1890, and the use of ornamental alabaster on a ceramic background—which can be seen on the door-posts—are of great interest from an architectural point of view.

Leaving the Patio de los Arrayanes by the north side one comes to the Sala de la Barca, which was it seems originally extensively decorated, but ·

*A corner of the Salón Dorado in the
Torre de Comares.*

unfortunately very little of this now remains.

The Patio de los Leones (The Courtyard of the Lions) is perhaps the most popular and widely known of the features of the Alhambra. It is in the centre of the collection of buildings forming the Palacio del Harem, the private residence of the Nazarite Kings and their large retinue of wives, concubines and children. It is an evocative place which stirs the imagination and gives rise to many flights of fancy.

The solid appearance of the twelve lions grouped round the stylized central fountain contrasts with the apparent fragility of the rest of the Alhambra, but combines with the over all design of the patio to give a most pleasing effect.

One cannot help admiring the beauty of the surrounding arches supported on their slender columns. This patio is an unique creation of incomparable personality.

The ancient basin of the fountain is made of white marble and around it are engraved some of the beautiful words composed by the poet Aben Zemrec for Mohammed V, in whose reign the Palacio del Harem was built—"By good fortune, in this garden have we not got something which God himself could not have wished more beautiful? It is decorated with pearls of great splendour and round the base there are even more pearls which seem to have overflowed from it. The silver water gushes between these

The play of light in the Patio de los Leones creates a fantasy which brings out the poetry of its architecture.

A close-up of six of the twelve magnificent lions which surround the white marble fountain.

The Patio de los Leones, as seen through the slender columns which surround it.

jewels and contrasts with the beauty of the white and gleaming marble." Among the buildings which make up the Harem and surround this marvellous patio is the famous Hall of the Lions, considered to be one of the most representative works of Moorish art in Granada.

Here the architecture blends harmoniously with the surrounding natural elements of air, water and light. It is a determined and successful attempt to humanize the severe geometrical designs which the architects of the Alhambra had previously imposed in an arbitrary manner. Now, in the XIV Century, the latent Christian ideas have become absorbed into Moslem Spain and the result is the marvellous jewel of Arab art which is the Alhambra.

A view through filigreed arches of the fountain, guarded by its lions.

Another view of the Patio de los Leones, seen in perspective.

The Sala de los Abencerrajes, the scene of tragic events in the Alhambra in Moorish times.

This picture of the Sala de las dos Hermanas shows the beauty of the decorated plaster.

One of the most delightful places in the Alhambra is without doubt the Mirador de Lindaraja which is found in the Sala de los Ajimeces. This chamber is, in fact, the first of the harem itself, and is decorated with exquisite delicacy, as also are the other adjoining rooms used by the Sultana.

At the back of the Mirador de Lindaraja there is an opening in the wall which leads to the special feature of a small tower with a view of the garden of the same name. It is an enchanting corner and is full of feminine coquetry.

The walls are tastefully embellished and those parts which are tiled have outstanding beauty. The floor is also tiled.

On the inside of the door-posts of one of the arches of the Mirador is engraved, in Arab characters, this poem of eulogy: "Each one of the arts has enriched me with its special beauty and endowered me with splendour and perfection. Everyone who sees me thinks, because of my beauty, of the wife to whom this chamber is dedicated and where are sought her favours. And when he gives his full attention to my splendour his eyes are blinded by the sight. Then, on catching sight of my splendid floor, he must surely think that the full moon resides here, having abandoned her house for mine."

From this delightful interior one looks out over a square garden with two side arches and one double arch.

The filigree work in the Mirador de Lindaraja gives it the appearance of a rich jewel casket.

An enchanting view of the fountain in the garden of Lindaraja.

The Sala de los Baños, also called the Sala del Reposo.

Another important chamber in the Harem is that of the Royal Baths. It is entered from the side of the Jardín de Lindaraja—which one can see from the Mirador of the same name—and is gaily painted and of genuine Arab style. In the centre of the Sala de los Baños there is a tiny fountain and everything here is most inviting—the quiet, the freshness and the clever filtering of the light. It is a most pleasing place in which to relax. The Sala de los Abencerrajes, apart from the interest of its unusual structure with its elegant capitals and the gay little chamber which crowns it, has a blood stained legend. It is said that it was in this room that Muley Abul Hasán had all his children by his first wife assassinated so that the throne would be inherited by the son of his favourite, Zoraya. This terrible story lives on today and people will tell you that certain rusty stains on the fountain are none other than the indellible stains of blood shed in this parricidal crime. Another legend asserts that several Abencerraje gentlemen were murdered here by order of Mohammed X.

A corner of the artistic stairway leading to the Sala de los Baños.

A majestic view of the Sala de los Reyes.

A delightful painting which decorates the ceiling in the Sala de los Reyes.

In the Alhambra one surprise follows another. Just when one believes that it is not possible to come across any further marvel, there springs up unexpectedly something new and exciting in the form of a patio or an apartment.

Such is the emotional atmosphere that when the power of the physical beauty is at last exhausted there is still something more to appeal to the imagination. For example, the unusual feature that in the central alcove of the Sala de los Reyes there is painted on the vaulted roof a picture of the Moslem rulers united in assembly and seated on luxurious cushions. Bearing in mind that, in accordance with the teaching of the Koran, Moslem art never depicts the human figure, it may legitimately be supposed that the paintings here are the work of a Christian artist.

Finally one must visit the Sala de las Dos Hermanas— which is on the opposite side to the Mirador de Lindaraja— and look at the two great slabs on either side of the small central fountain and admire the skilful composition of masses and the perfect illumination of this chamber. Now the time has come to go out into the fresh air and make one's way to the poetical Jardines del Partal.

If you go out by the Patio de los Leones, you can first inspect the Royal Cemetery —La Rauda— from where Boabdil, the las King of Granada, had the remains of his ancestors removed and taken to Mondújar.

The Jardines del Partal have been restored with absolute respect to the design of its original creators. They are surrounded by many interesting monuments whose outlines are of pure Arab origin and are reflected in the water of the central pool.

The Court of Lions, after a 19th-century engraving.

The most important of the buildings in this part of the Alhambra is, without doubt, El Partal or, as it is more usually called, La Torre de las Damas. It rises up behind the gardens, proudly surveying the land around. It is said that it was from this tower that Boabdil escaped after he had decided to confront his father, Muley Abul Hasán, King of Granada, infatuated by the beauty of Zoraya.

Its original name came from the gate — Partal — formed by the five access arches to the tower. It has also been called Torre del Príncipe and Baño de las Odaliscas.

The gallery of the Torre de las Damas has an ornamental ceiling which is entirely made of wood and with very original work on it. In the centre there is a cupola adorned with stars, small domes and curved shells. Half-a-dozen small balconies open out at one end of the gallery which also has triple arches on each side. A larger arch leads to the main hall with three windows on each wall. Here there are inscribed these verses:

¡Salve, oh mansión! Que la alegría y la dicha revoloteen en torno a ti ayudadas por el poder y la esperanza. / Que tu puerta obtenga en ti tus deseos y que

A romantic picture of the beautiful gardens of the Partal.

sea continuamente acompañada por lo que él, tu dueño, espera. Que su noche sea en ti agradable, toda ella aurora y que su día sea risueño por la continuidad de la alegría en su rostro. Que no deje de proteger y de hacer triunfar al reino y que el poder, la suerte y los cambios del Destino estén a su servicio.

From the belvedere, which is the highest part of the tower, one can see a delightful view of the valley of the Darro. Two large stone lions stand on guard beside the pool of the Partal. One leaves the Torre de las Damas — whose construction is thought to date from the early part of the XIV Century — with feelings of melancholy.

To the right of that of Las Damas stands the Torre del Mihrab, the parapet of the wall serving as its base. The façade is in the form of a horse-shoe shaped arch, and inside there is an unusual Oratorio of Moslem style.

After inspecting the tower of Los Picos, built to defend one of the en-

The silhouettes of the cypress trees lend this view of the Partal a melancholy air.

The five graceful arches of the portico of the Torre de las Damas cast their reflections over the water of the pool.

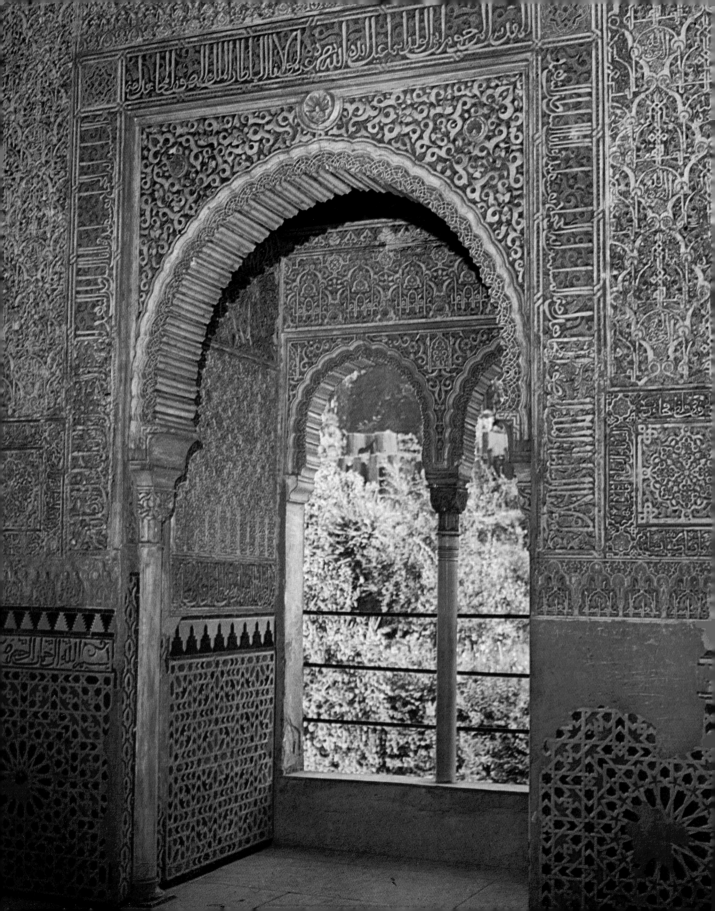

A corner of the Torre de la Cautiva.

The renaissance façade of the Palace of Carlos V impresses by the strength of its architectural design.

trances of the fortress which gave on to the Generalife, the tower of the Cadí—formerly named the Pres—and that of Las Infantas, you ought to stop and look at that of the Cautiva built by Yusuf I. It has delicate plaster work and evokes the romantic figure of Doña Isabel de Solís, who was no other than the beautiful Zoraya whose poetic legend lingers on throughout the Alhambra. Having seen such a great Arab marvel and reconstructed in one's mind the whole atmosphere of the Alhambra, it might help to dispel your mixed feelings if you went to inspect the façade of the old monastery of San Francisco, a Moorish palace of the late XIV Century and today a Parador Nacional de Turismo. In the great chapel were buried the Catholic Monarchs.

The serene majesty of the Palace of Carlos V stands in striking contrast to the graceful Moorish Architecture of the Alhambra.

The restrained elegance of Renaissance architecture is perfectly reflected by Pedro Machuca in the magnificent circular patio in the palace of Carlos V.

This beautiful pitcher from the Alhambra can be seen in the National Museum of Spanish-Moslem Art in Granada.

THE PALACE OF CARLOS V

Among the many fine buildings over which the Alhambra presides, the Renaissance Palace of Carlos V is one of the most remarkable. It began to be built in the year 1527 under the direction of Pedro Machuca, and was destined to be the residence of the Emperor who had a special fondness for Granada. The work however had to be suspended in 1568 because of the Moorish rebellion and could not be resumed until the year 1579.

The Palace is in the form of a quadrangle and has an air of serene majesty. It is considered to be the most beautiful Renaissance palace existing outside Italy.

The south front boasts a magnificent porch, artistically decorated by the sculptor Nicolao da Corte, and the west front has some important carvings by Juan de Orea.

The central patio, which is circular, is of impressive size and is totally surrounded by a spacious colonnade of pillars in the Doric style. These make a contrast with the Ionic columns in the gallery above.

The Palace of Carlos V has an authentic aristocratic presence and its Renaissance style gives it an undeniable impression of architectural majesty.

To go from the ethereal and romantic atmosphere of the Alhambra to the classical restraint shown in the Palacio de Carlos V is an abrupt but rewarding experience.

A wonderful view of the city taken from the Torre de las Damas.

The Museo Nacional de Arte Hispano-Musulman is housed on the ground floor of the Palacio de Carlos V and has a rich collection of Moorish and Mudéjar work. Perhaps the most important piece is the famous Pitcher of the Alhambra — El Jarrón de la Alhambra — which for a long period was on show in the Sala de las dos Hermanas. Its Moorish grace is equalled only by the delicacy of its decoration. ·

The stone water trough from the XI Century is also very valuable and has magnificent reliefs showing lions and antelopes fighting at the foot of a tree. The tombs, capitals, arches and examples of Arab ceramic work are of great interest.

Other outstanding Arab pieces are an extremely beautiful dish, on which appears a bird mounted on a horse — this comes from Medina Elvira — and a pair of bracelets made of engraved and embossed gold.

The Museum also possesses a most interesting collection of examples of Visgothic art, such as bracelets, ear-rings of bronce and silver, delicate necklaces of chrystal and amber, rings, clasps of bronze from the IV and V Centuries and a number of Corinthian capitals.

A very fine carved stone cistern, one of the most valuable treasures in the collection of the Museum of Spanish-Moslem Art, housed in the Palace of Carlos V.

Triptych of the Gran Capitán in raised enamel, a work of great artistic value.

THE PROVINCIAL MUSEUM OF FINE ARTS

This Museum is on the first storey of the Palacio de Carlos V. Formerly it was in the Casa de Castril which belonged to Don Hernando de Zafra, the secretary to the Catholic Monarchs.

The present home of the Museum is spacious and provides an ideal setting. It was inaugurated in the year 1958 and consists of eleven rooms together with entrance and exit halls which house a rich

"Expulsión de los judíos sefardíes" – *"The Expulsion of the Spanish Jews "* – *by Emilio Sala, hanging in the Museo de Bellas Artes in Granada.*

"Virgen con el Niño en brazos", *a magnificent carving by Diego de Siloé.*

A valuable Flemish tapestry hanging in one of the halls of the Museum of Granada.

and varied picture gallery and a valuable collection of sculpture.

One of the most important works in this Musuem is the central panel of the Tríptico del Gran Capitán, a fine enamel from Limoges which dates from the 15th century and is attributed to Nardon Penicaud.

Outstanding among the paintings are a number of large pictures dealing with religious subjects by Juan de Sevilla, some impressive canvases of Pedro Antonio Bocanegra, a panel representing the Virgin and Child — an example of Spanish-Flemish art of the 15th century — the notable collection of works by Sánchez Cotán, a Lucas Giordano and an interesting selection of canvases and panels by unknown painters.

Nineteenth-century painting is represented by the works of Madrazo, Muñoz Degrain, Gómez Moreno, Pérez Villamil, Vicente López, Carlos

"La Virgen despertando al Niño", a delightful painting by the monk, Juan Sánchez.

"Espadero toledano" - "The Toledan Swordsmith" - a work of vigorous realism by Mariano Fortuny.

"Después del trabajo", an expressive painting by Martínez Cubells.

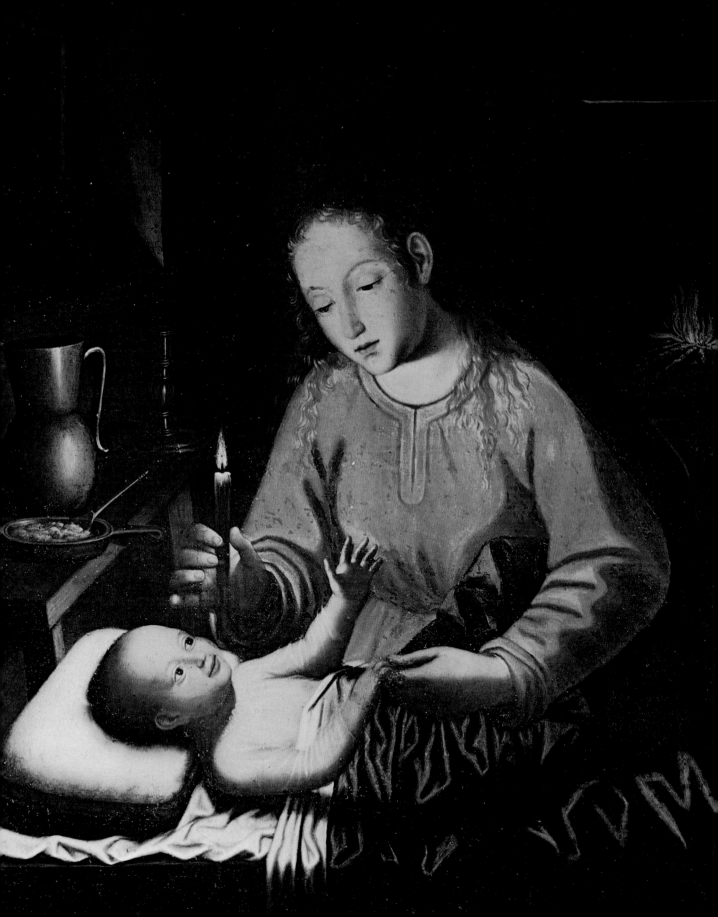

Haes, Moreno Carbonero, José Larrocha, Emilio Sala, Fortuny and Martínez Cubells.

Among 20th-century painters the best represented are Rodríguez Acosta, Luis Mosquera, Roberto, Domingo, Gómez Mir, Soria Aedo and Vázquez Díaz.

The famous Salón de la Chimenea Italiana (Salon of the Italian chimney-piece) is of special interest. It is a spacious room in which the restraint and good taste shown in the decoration results in perfect harmony. It takes its name from the beautiful marble chimney-piece which was made in the made in the 16th century in Italy and was destined for the Palacio de Carlos V.

It is pleasant and soothing to wander through the rooms of Granada's Museum of Fine Arts. After the fascination of seeing the marvellous world of the Alhambra with all its glamorous history, a stroll through the Palacio de Carlos V followed by a visit to its two museums brings a feeling of peace.

At first the imagination has become intoxicated by the story of this fantastic country, inhabited by exciting houris and filled with illusions of magic and splendour, but now everything is calm — one has regained control and returned to reality. In a very short space of time an incredible distance in history has been covered — the distance that separates the Moslem world from the Christian world — and those two worlds have entirely different conceptions of life.

The elegant Salón de la Chimenea Italiana.

The sculptural exhibits in the Museo de Bellas Artes of Granada are very fine. Of particular interest is a decorated carving of great size on wood called "Entierro de Cristo" (The burial of Christ). The author is Jacobo Florentino. Other valuable works are; the "Virgen con el Niño" – a polichromed carving attributed to Roberto Alemán, the "Virgen con el Niño en los brazos" by Diego Siloé, the splendid "Cabeza de San Juan de Dios" by Alonso Cano, the moving "Ecce-Homo" (Behold the Man) of Pedro de Mena, the four large sculptures carved in collaboration by Alonso Cano and Pedro de Mena, the "San Mateo" of Juan de Orea and the "Niño Jesús en Oración" by Risueño.

"Los charros", an oil by Soria Aedo. ▷

"El coleo", by Roberto Domingo.

"La gitana", by
Rodríguez Acosta.

*An unusual portrait
of the novelist Pío Baroja,
without his
characteristic beret,
painted by
Luis Mosquera.*

"La Alpujarra", an oil
by Gómez Mir.

A view of the wonderful Patio de la Acequia, in the Generalife.

THE GENERALIFE

The palace and gardens of the Generalife are situated on the slopes of the Cerro del Sol from which there is a splendid view, dominated by the city of Granada, of the valleys of the Darro and the Genil.

The Generalife was formerly a pleasure palace of the Kings of Granada, and its name is derived, according to all the available evidence, from *Gennat-Alarif*, which means "the garden of the architect". It was probably built in the middle of the 13th century but since then it has been altered on a number of occasions.

The beauty and enchantment of these gardens are unrivalled, and the many walks invite one to dream. The Paseo de los Cipreses and the Paseo de las Adelfas seem to lead to some romantic secret sanctuary.

Here in the Patio de la Acequia the scent of the flowers and the soft mur-

Fountains, flowers, myrtles and cypress trees personify the poetical melancholy which hangs over the gardens of the Generalife.

A pair of tall cypresses stand guard over the slow passage of the watercourse flowing from the Generalife.

mur of the water from the fountains produce the illusion that one is in a land of fairy tales.

The ethereal outline of the little palace, as it gazes at its reflection in the mirror of the pool, seems to be saying that here dwells a prince crowned with melancholy.

Everything in the palace is neat and simple. Among the archways, the chambers, the galleries and the plaster lattices hovers a twilight grace. The decoration is superb, and through the carefully-placed belvederes, subtly filtering the view, appears the landscape with the shyness of a young girl.

In the Patio de la Sultana stands a large and ancient cypress tree. It is not difficult to imagine, surrounded by all these evocative memories, that it is hiding the furtive figure of an Arab King, bearing in his bosom the scorpion of jealousy as he lies in wait for a beautiful slave girl.

The design of the gardens of the Generalife is highly individual. The unusual lay-out is delineated by an enchanting labyrinth of bowers, fountains, flower-beds, a veritable paradise of geraniums and carnations and green hedges of box and cypress.

The enchanting views to be seen from the many marvellous belvederes keep changing like the slides in a magic lantern and remain indelibly imprinted on the memory.

A lovely corner of the Generalife.

The ancient entrance to the Chapel Royal now inside the Cathedral of Granada.

The exterior and main entrance of the Chapel Royal.

THE ROYAL CHAPEL

Following the entrance of the Catholic Monarchs into Granada—a great historical event which took place on the second of January 1492—there started in the city an artistic and cultural movement of the first importance. Thus began a period of the Renaissance which was splendidly portrayed in this ancient capital of the Kingdom of Granada.

The special warmth of feeling that Isabel the Catholic always felt towards Granada made her decide, according to the royal decree signed in Medina del Campo on the thirteenth of September 1504, to

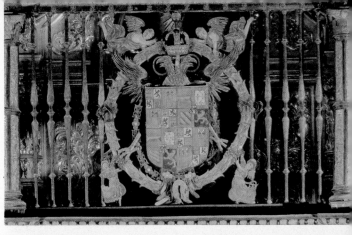

The Chapel Royal: the Reja del Perdón (Railing of Forgiveness), detail of the railing of the Chapel of Santa Cruz, and detail of the railing of the high altar.

The Lonja or Exchange House.

*Statues of the Catholic Monarchs in
prayer, in the sacristy of the Chapel Royal.
The coffins of the Catholic Monarchs.*

*The crown, sceptre and coffer of
Isabel the Catholic, and the sword of
King Ferdinand.*

The Plateresque reredos of the High Altar, one of the first in this style, the work of Felipe de Vigarny.

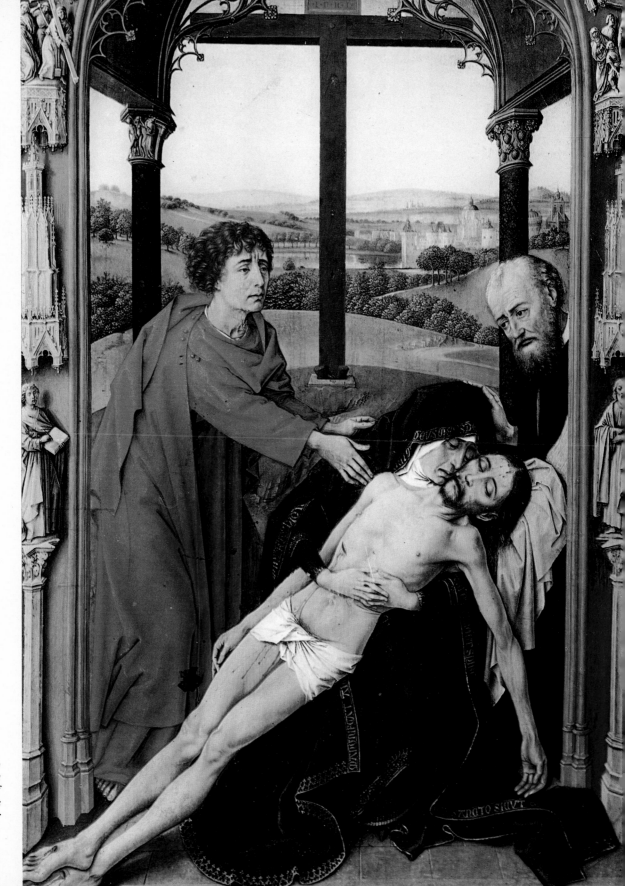

"Virgin with Child", a beautiful oil by Dierick Bouts.

"Cristo muerto" a painting of deep pathos by Van der Weyden.

build the famous Chapel Royal as a sepulchre for the bodies of herself and her husband. The work was begun under the direction of Enrique Egas in the year 1506. Queen Isabel had by then already died and her remains laid to rest provisionally in the convent of San Francisco. King Ferdinand took special care to comply with his wife's wishes and, on his death on the twenty third of January 1516, his body was also taken to Granada to rest beside his Queen in the same convent. On the tenth of November 1521 both were removed to the Chapel Royal, where their tombs remain to this day.

The chapel is built in the style of Toledo with a pronounced ogival influence, and is a typical example of the architecture during the reign of the Catholic Monarchs.

Outside, the Chapel has only one façade. This is due to the fact that on its other three sides the building adjoins the walls of the cathedral, the church of the Sagrario and the Lonja (The Exchange).

This front aspect is restrained and has a portico in Plateresque style. The walls, which are flanked by buttresses ending in decorative pinnacles, support pierced balustrades with fine crests. The poised elegance of the great windows and the gargoyles combine harmoniously with the shields and emblems of the Catholic Monarchs which enoble the façade of the Chapel.

The transept is enclosed by an artistic gilt screen of Plateresque style and is a fine example of the work of Bartolomé de Jaén.

The tombs of the Catholic Monarchs and of Joan the Mad and Philip the Fair, sculpted in marble from Carrara.

On the other side of this screen are the royal tombs. They are sculptured in Carrara marble, and beside them are the tombs of Felipe el Hermoso and Juana la Loca, the daughter of the Catholic Monarchs.

The four bodies, together with that of Miguel the boy prince, lie below in the crypt enclosed in metal coffins of impressive austerity.

The magnificent reredos behind the High Altar is the work of Vigarny. It is one of the first of the Plateresque altar screens to be made in Spain, but one can see various additions in ogival style.

The two other altars are also worth seeing and have reredoses in the form of cupboards. These contain the relics given by several Popes to the Catholic Monarchs who donated them to the Chapel Royal.

The valuable treasures of the Chapel have since 1945 been kept in the Sacristy, over which is placed a XVI Century figure of Christ with statues

"Cristo", a fine work by Perugino.

"Oración del Huerto", a delicate painting by Botticelli, hanging in the picture gallery of the Chapel Royal of Granada.

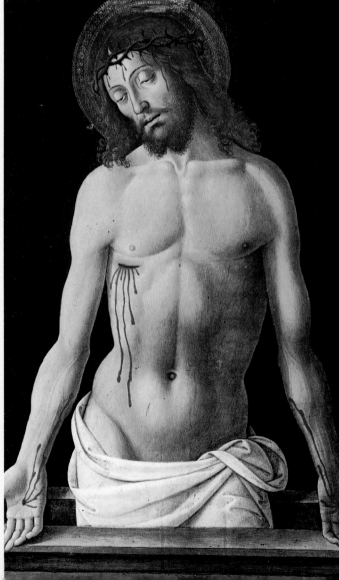

*A fragment from the "Santas mujeres",
an unusual painting by Memling.*

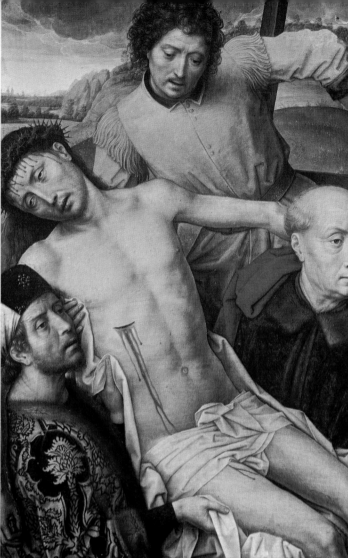

"San Juan Evangelista", an original painting by Berruguete.

"Descendimiento", by Memling.

of the Catholic Monarchs kneeling in prayer at his feet. These treasures consist of jewels of immense value, and three of the most outstanding are the crown and sceptre of Queen Isabel and the sword of King Ferdinand.

Other important items are the Queen's coffer—which according to tradition and popular legend once held the jewels sold to help finance Christopher Columbus—her gilded silver mirror, now converted into a monstrance, an altar cross, a chalice with engraved decoration and a splendid pyx with relief work in marble.

Another valuable part of the treasure is the collection of paintings, in which there are canvases signed by Botticceli, Perugino, Van der Weyden, Memling, Bouts, Berruguete and El Bosco.

A visit to the Chapel Royal evokes memories of the past and creates a series of spiritual and historical images which help towards a fuller understanding of the complex spirit of Granada.

THE CATHEDRAL

Some four months after the conquest of Granda by the Christian armies the first Cathedral in Granada was installed in the Mosque of the Alhambra. Later it was moved to the monastery of San Francisco, and later still it was decided to erect the final building of the Cathedral beside the Great Mosque which by that time had been converted into the church of Santa María de la O.

The work was begun in 1518. At first it was planned to build to a Gothic design, similar to the Cathedral at Toledo, but later this project was abandoned, and in 1528 Diego Siloé took charge and directed the work until his death in 1563.

The principal façade is the work of Alonso Cano who modified and simplified Siloé's original plan.

The Cathedral is a building where miracles can happen, and in every part there is wonder and delight.

The triptych of the Passion, a magnificent piece by Dierick Bouts.

The main
Chapel of the
Cathedral,
one of Siloé's
major works.

An aerial view
of Granada,
with the
Cathedral in
the
foreground.

The head of
St. John the
Baptist, the
work of Ruiz
del Peral.

The Virgin of
Bethlehem, a
delightful
sculpture by
Alonso Cano.

The architectural grandeur of the Basilica of Granada is impressive, A surprising feature of its design is that on top of a Gothic floor plan there has later been developed a Renaissance building, and all this has been done without the result being out of harmony.

The interior of the Cathedral is astonishing in its magnificence. It consists of five naves of huge dimensions, and the whole area seems, on both sides, to be filled with chapels in which one can see beautiful retables and valuable works by Alonso Cano, Torrigiano, Bocanegra and Ribera.

The whole area is filled with light because of the many windows which open into the chapels. The stained glass windows which have been preserved are very beautiful, especially the seven Flemish windows which are the work of Teodoro de Holanda and represent scenes in the life of the Virgin, and the three showing the Holy Parents, painted by Jan Campen.

The interior of the Cathedral is painted white, and against the white background of the walls there is the contrast of the shining gold of the main chapel, the masterly work of Diego de Siloé. On the Plateresque columns of the main arch one can see statues of the Catholic Monarchs in prayer, sculptured by Pedro de Mena and Medrano. A little higher up are two magnificent busts of Adam and Eve, the work of Alonso Cano and polichromed by Vélez de Ulloa.

The Puerta del Perdón, the finest entrance to the Cathedral of Granada.

A view of the dazzling Gilded Chapel of the Cathedral.

*The interior
of the
Cathedral
seems filled
with majestic
light.*

THE MONASTERY OF SAN JERONIMO

Founded by the Catholic Monarchs in Santa Fe in 1492 the Monasterio de San Jerónimo was dedicated to Santa Catalina and transferred immediately to Granada. Work on the building was begun in 1496 and completed under the direction of Siloé in 1547. For the building of this monastery the Catholic Monarchs donated all the Arab stone from the Puerta de Elvira.

The monastery which possessed many valuable ornaments was sacked by the French and later converted into barracks, but some years ago it was restored with the help of the University of Granada and the Order of San Jerónimo.

The patios and gardens are exceptionally beautiful as also are the cloisters. The front of the church boasts an unusual decoration. It is the work of Siloé and consists of the shield of the Catholic Monarchs beneath a window encased in an arch which has carvings of fantastic animals. Over the four Doric columns of the porch is a small shrine with a statue of Saint Francis.

The large reredos in the main chapel is of unusual interest. It is made in such a way that it extends from the front of the apse to the vault behind, and high up there are four figures which stand out from the valuable carved panels.

A study of the magnificent reredos in the Church of San Jerónimo.

Statues of the Gran Capitán and his wife María Manrique in prayer, to be seen in the Monastery of San Jerónimo.

The beautiful Plateresque entrance to the Cartuja of Granada.

THE CARTHUSIAN MONASTERY

Situated on the outskirts of the city, the Carthusian Monastery (La Cartuja) is of a formal architectural design and has an attractive Plateresque portico, which is earlier than those of the Chapel Royal and the Lonja, with a semi-circular arch bearing the Arms of Spain. Pillars on each side support a simply decorated cornice, above which in an embellished vaulted niche stands a XVI Century statue of the Virgin carved in wood.

Behind lies the church and a large courtyard, and at one side is the entrance to the Monastery, reached by stairs made of Elvira stone.

Part of the cloister of the Cartuja.

The Refectory of the Cartuja, built mid-sixteenth century.

The Lay Choirstalls in the Cartuja with two splendid paintings by Sánchez Cotán.

The walls of the Claustrillo—a delightful patio with Doric arches—were originally decorated with pictures by Vicente Carducho and Sánchez Cotán but which now hang in the Refectory.

Between the two altars there is an unusual door encrusted with ivory, shells and rare woods.

The two choirs—the monk's choir and the lay choir—communicate by way of another attractive door. Here one can see pictures by Bocanegra and Sánchez Cotán showing religious scenes.

In the Refectory one's attention is drawn to the ogival vaults and a cross painted by Sánchez Cotán on a rock. By the same artist is the retable in the Sala de Profundis.

The church is entirely made of stone. Behind the altar and the chancel—which acts as the sanctuary—is the outstanding Sancta Sanctorum where one can admire a shrine with vivid baroque decoration. A door on the left leads to the sacristy, a room which surprises with the subtlety of its lines. It is a veritable idealization of the baroque style. The audacious mixing of different decorative elements is dazzling. Here one can say that there is a display of baroque extravagance intensified by the interplay between the effects of the light and the perspective.

The sacristy of the Cartuja was completed in the year 1764.

A partial view of the sacristy, showing the rich decoration.

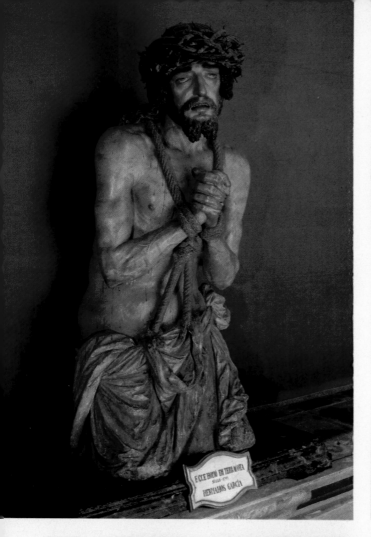

Terracotta Ecce Homo, attributed to the García brothers, and conserved in the Cartuja.

The Virgin of the Rosary, by Bocanegra, also to be found in the Cartuja.

St. Bruno, a magnificent figurine by José de Mora, on display in the Cartuja.

THE HOSPITAL OF SAN JUAN DE DIOS

The hospital stands beside the church of San Juan de Dios and occupies the ancient monastery of San Jerónimo—that beautiful example of Spanish Renaissance architecture founded by the Catholic Monarchs in 1492 and moved to its present site in 1504.

The Nursing Order of San Juan de Dios founded the hospital, which has a fine portico with Doric columns and the interesting feature of a magnificent ceiling over the stairway. Standing in the Calle de San Juan de Dios, its life and work are closely linked with the city of Granada.

The magnificent patio of the hospital of San Juan de Dios with its beautiful surrounding arches.

THE CHURCH OF SAN JUAN DE DIOS

The building of this church was started in 1737 and it was consecrated in 1759. It is one of the most beautiful places of worship in Granada. The façade is surmounted by two high towers topped by spires and the entrance is of marble from the Sierra Elvira with mahogany doors. This was designed by José Bada and has two sections of columns set on pedestals. One section is Corinthian and the other Composite. In the centre of the higher section stands a statue of San Juan de Dios, the work of Ramiro Ponce de León.

The plan of the church is in the form of a Latin cross. Inside there are four small chapels, a choir and a dome at the crossing of the naves. The main chapel has an impressive gilded reredos with fine gold decoration, the work of J.F. Guerrero. One's attention is immediately caught by the rich shrine in the centre of the reredos with its profusion of reliefs, paintings, marble ornaments and mirrors.

The Capilla Mayor of the church of San Juan de Dios dazzles with its richness of ornamentation.

This picture by Gómez-Moreno symbolizes the spirit which illuminated the life and work of San Juan de Dios.

The façade of the church of San Juan de Dios, showing the Baroque entrance and the towers topped with spires.

THE CITY

History has had a profound effect on Granada. The city has been the crucible of differing cultures and the meeting place of race and religion, and all the resulting economic and social changes have left their mark. These great events of history and the geographical position of Granada have conditioned and moulded the character of its people. They are more introverted and quieter than Andalusians in general, but also they have a certain courtesy. Théofile Gautier, the French writer who loved the glow and fire of Andalusians, lived for some time in Granada, in the Calle Párraga, and there developed his creative genius.

Granada is without doubt one of most beautiful cities in Spain, and has the advantage of a delightful climate—the logical consequence of its ideal situation, looking out over a fruitful plain and almost at the foot of the Sierra Nevada. As García Lorca has said:—*Los dos ríos de Granada bajan de la nieve al trigo.*

A general view of Granada with the Cathedral in the centre.

A peaceful view of the street leading to the Cathedral and the Chapel Royal.

Façade of la Madraza.

Modern Granada extends over the plain, whereas the ancient town with its Jewish and Moorish roots clung to the hills presided over by the Alhambra.

The centre of the city is where the two main thoroughfares intersect; the Gran Vía de Colón — out of which runs the street leading to the Chapel Royal and the Cathedral — and the Avenida de los Reyes Católicos.

It is a real pleasure to lose oneself in any of the delightful side streets, such as the purely Arab Alcaicería or the Zacatín, or perhaps relax in the popular Plaza de Bibarrambla. Also worthy of note is the Plaza de Isabel la Católica, at the junction of the calle de los Reyes Católicos and the Gran Vía de Colón, with its beautiful fountain and the statue of Queen Isabel I, and further down the Plaza is joined by the street of Angel Ganivet, the ill-fated writer from Granada who was the author of the famous work entitled "Idearium Español". The unique character of Granada permeates the whole city and makes it one of the most beautiful and individual in Spain.

Coffered ceiling of the oratory of the Arab Room of la Madraza.

Detail of the oratory in the Arab Room (La Madraza).

The oratory in the Arab Room (La Madraza).

The Knights' Room.

Close-up view of the Virgin of the Rose, by an unknown hand.

The Fuente del Triunfo at dusk (pages 92/93).

Plaza Nueva (New Square).

Monument to the Catholic Queen Isabella and Columbus.

Partial view of the Plaza de Bibarrambla.

The Alcaicería.

The beautiful entrance patio of the Royal Hospital.

Two delightful corners of the gardens of the Fundación Rodríguez Acosta, near the Palace of Carlos V.

The Casa de Castril. The doorway, though attributed to Siloé, seems to be the work of Sebastián de Alcántara.

THE TOWN HALL

Today the Town Hall of Granada is housed in part of the Monastery of the Carmelitas Calzados which survived the dissolution. The building has been altered from time to time and in 1910 it was extended as far as the Calle de Los Reyes Católicos.

Inside the building—the centre of which is the ancient patio of the former monastery—there is an interesting Historical Museum founded in 1939, where is preserved the Treaty of the "Surrender of Granada by the Arabs" signed by the Catholic Monarchs. Here also are the city's shield—a valuable coloured embroidery which Queen Isabel the Catholic gave to the Council of Granada in 1493—the Royal Standard of Granada with the shield of the Austrias embroidered on carmine damask, a XVI Century tapestry with a picture of the Virgin, an example of the Gothic text of the Statutes of the city, the Patents in which Isable II granted to Granada the title "Heroic" and a number of elegant silver pieces.

The Museum also contains a small wooden chest—with allegorical decorations—in which lie the remains of Mariana Pineda, the girl from Granada who inspired one of García Lorca's first theatrical works, and the manuscript of the poem by Zorrilla entitled "Los gnomos de la Alhambra".

Among the paintings beloging to the Town Hall the most interesting are a picture by Juan Leandro de la Puente, signed in 1639, re-

The luxurious Salón de Sesiones in Granada's Town Hall.

*The elegant
mantelpiece
of the Salón de
Sesiones.*

presenting the Fiesta de Pentecostés (the Feast of Pentecost), a crucifixion and a "Piedad" the work of Gómez-Moreno, a portrait of Isabel II by Soledad Enríquez, one of Mariana Pineda—the threshold of her tragic destiny—by J. Lozano, another of Alfonso XII by Madrazo, pictures of Castelar, Cánovas del Castillo and Sagasta by Gómez-Moreno, and other valuable works signed by Isidoro Marín, José M.ª López Mezquita and Gabriel Morcillo.

The Municipal Archives have a very interesting collection of historical documents which enables one to follow, step by step, the illustrious course of Christian Granada. Here are kept the Minute Books of the city since 1497, thirteen books of Privileges and Royal Letters Patent from 1490 and a valuable collection of Royal Charters and Decrees with the autographed signatures of the Catholic Monarchs and successive monarchs of great historical value. The nearby wide and busy Avenida de los Reyes Católicos lends an air of importance to the Town Hall.

The Treaty of Surrender signed by Boabdil.

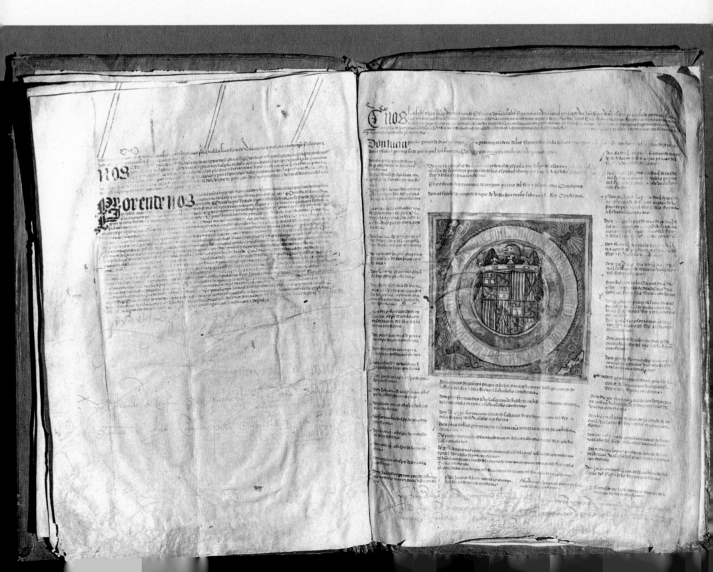

The fine craftmanship of Granada, started in Moorish times and
continuing till the present day, has a world-wide reputation. Here are
four examples. A piece of Ceramic ware, marquetry work, some
valuable rugs and a craftsman making a guitar.

THE HOUSE OF THE TIROS

Standing in the Calle de Pavaneras the Casa de los Tiros— once the palace of the Princes of Granada—contains the Head Office of the Tourist Department and a well-stocked Museum of the history of the city.

The building has the appearance of a fortress, and it is said that it was originally part of the walls which protected the district of the Alfareros.

The present Casa de los Tiros was built in the first half of the XVI Century. The whole of the front aspect is of stone and ends in a square fortified tower topped by battlements and a roof which was added in the XIX Century.

There is a simple doorway with a lintel in the centre, a couple of balconies and five statues depicting Hercules, Theseus, Jason, Hector and Mercury. The latter bears on his heraldic clothing the Arms of the House.

The ground floor is occupied by a spacious and impressive entrance hall with the great beams of the roof supported by Gothic lintels. On the walls of the adjoining passageways one can see interesting panels with paintings of battles between wild animals and imaginary beasts.

The patio is quite small and contains a number of Moorish capitals and columns. The most interesting room is, without doubt, the main chamber which retains today its original architectural purity with

The original front of the Casa de los Tiros reveals that once it was a fortress.

Coffered ceiling of the Cuadra Doráda (Golden Hall) in the Casa de los Tiros.

artistically carved beams and lintels with beautiful reliefs. Four stone medallions, with busts in high relief, decorate the upper part of the walls, and on the doors are magnificent carvings in Plateresque style.

The varied treasure of the museum of the Casa de los Tiros was first collected by Antonio Gallego y Burín, an illustrious son of Granada, who was Director General of Fine Arts and whose portrait now hangs in one of the rooms. Throughout one can sense the subtle presence of the soul of Granada and the complex and varied personality of a city steeped in history. On the ground floor, beside the patio, there is a kitchen in the style of Alpujarras with a typical primitive hearth adorned with pieces of ceramic ware and other domestic utensils, and an example of the interior of an inn in the Sierra Nevada, at the time of the Duke of San Pedro de Galatino. Another room contains bull-fighting trophies connected with Granada and an interesting album of press cuttings from 1764.

On the floor above, the Museum offers a wide range of artistic and historical works of various kinds. Here are represented outstanding and contrasting personalities of Granada such as, for example; —the Empress Eugenie who has a room dedicated to her memory; a portrait of the ill-fated Mariana Pineda and three pictures of her progress towards her execution at the scaffold; and pictures of "Chorroejumo" the King of the gypsies, the writers Martínez de la Rosa and Pedro Antonio Alarcón, and General Alvarez de Castro who defended Gerona against Napoleon.

There is a room dedicated to Washington Irving, an American who chose to live in Granada, in which you can see many editions of his famous work "Tales of the Alhambra". This room also has a library of books about the Alhambra by both Spanish and foreign authors.

The atmosphere here is full of romance and the picture is completed by the presence of a harp and a piano.

The room dedicated to Washington Irving, the American writer who wrote the "Tales of the Alhambra".

Another room in the Museum — a dining-room in Spanish style — exhibits a magnificent collection of the ceramic ware of Granada. The pieces are hung on the walls and the whole room is arranged with excellent good taste so as to give a balanced view of the decorative art of Granada.

There are antique ceramic examples from Fajalauza which have great beauty and originality with designs in blue and green.

In contrast with the decoration of ceramic ware there are curtains from Alpujarras, XVII Century furniture, wrought-iron work and many valuable pieces of copper.

The Museum also has a rich collection of Court pictures, among which are portraits of the Catholic Monarchs — dating from the XVII Century — of Margarita of Austria, of Felipe IV, of Isabel de Borbón, of Felipe I, of Felipe II, of Don Juan of Austria, of Isabel de Farnesio and of Felipe V. Among all these the most outstanding is the portrait of Carlos V, an example of the work of Jerónimo de la Chica.

In this room the imagination is captured by effigies of Boabdil and Aben-Humeya and attractive prints of Moorish scenery.

The slim and graceful figure of the Empress Eugenie of Montijo gives a special meaning to the evocative atmosphere of the room dedicated to her. The life-sized statue is dressed in white with a crown and wearing a sash in the colours of the Spanish flag.

A beautiful picture of the dining-room of the Casa de los Tiros, profusely decorated with precious ceramic ware from Fajalauza.

The world of the gypsies also has its special place in the Casa de los Tiros.

Terracota figures in the Sala de los Gitanos (the room of the Gypsies).

A corner of the room dedicated to Eugenie of Montijo, the girl from Granada who became Empress of France.

A room full of documentary interest dealing with traditional customs is dedicated to the gypsies. The atmosphere is enlivened by the jaunty and rather ironical figure of Chorroejumo, the King of the gypsies, and there is a graceful statue of Rafaela, dexterously carved in marble by Juan Cristóbal. Here also is an unusual collection of works in terracota which reproduce scenes of gypsy life. The "Romancero Gitano" by García Lorca is full of comments about the world of the gypsies and their language (the Calé), and from its pages are taken the following lines:

> *Antonio Torres Heredia,*
> *hijo y nieto de Camborios,*
> *con una vara de mimbre*
> *va a Sevilla a ver los toros.*

The many examples of art from Granada on show in the various rooms of this building tell us, step by step, about this simple and aristocratic city, about its history and its craftmanship.

Entrance arch of the Casa de Carbón. This building, dating from the beginning of the 14th century, served as a warehouse for merchandise and as lodgings for Moorish merchants.

Patio of the Casa del Carbón (House of Coal).

Entrance arch to the Casa del Carbón, after a 19th-century engraving.

A beautiful panorama of the Albaicín as seen from the Alhambra.

THE ALBAICIN

The Albaicín is a popular district of unique personality and was under Arab rule, together with the Alcazaba, the most important centre of population in Granada. It stretches to the edge of the walls of the Alcazaba, and between, from the ridge of San Miguel on the one side to the gates of Huadix and Alacaba on the other.

The name of Albaicín probably comes from the fact that this part of the city was occupied by the Arabs who settled there in the year 1227, after having been driven our from Baeza by Ferdinand III, The Saint. Juan Rufo in his poem, "La Austriada", published in 1584, explains the change of spelling in the following lines:— *"Y por ser de Baeza naturales los más de los que el sitio edificaron, llamáronle Albaecin, y otros no tales la "e" y la "c" en "y" y "z" mudaron."*

Nevertheless, some researches, among them the Arab Aben Aljatib, consider that the name Albaicín means "the district on a slope or hill", which certainly suits the geographical location of this delightful part of Granada.

The Albaicín: the Church of St.
Bartholomew.

The Albaicín: Doorway of the Convent of
Santa Isabel la Real.

The Albaicín: Palace of Daralhorra or
Casa de la Reina.

However, there is no doubt that the Albaicín was one of the busiest centres of population in Moorish Granada, and this is confirmed by the fact that here there were some thirty mosques and many water-troughs and public fountains. Indeed some of these are still in existence today.

The people of Albaicín always had the reputation of being proud and rebellious. During the times of Arab rule they used to mount raids on neighbouring territories in search of booty, and later, when Granada had already been conquered by the Christians, they played an active part in the Moorish rebellion, which was led by Aben Humeya and ended in the deportation of the vanquished to the lands of Castille.

From this time began the decay of the Albaicín and the decline in its industrial activities, for the textiles of Granada had enjoyed a well-earned reputation in the Middle Ages.

Today the Albaicín is a part of the town which largely retains its primitive simplicity. The interior design of the houses brings back memories of its Moorish past, and the lay-out of the streets create a veritable labyrinth. The low houses cluster on the steep slopes beside irregular and narrow lanes which more often than not have no pavements. To walk through the Albaicín today is to experience a certain strange sensation—a feeling of being submerged in a forgotten world, a world still dreaming of

The classic charm of the "Cármenes", with its little houses and gardens, brings to the Albaicín a feeling of peace and Christian humility.

Two views of a typical Moorish house: one of its porch and the other of its patio.

A vigorous and impressive statue of Christ on the Cross in the Plaza de San Miguel el Bajo.

mystery and romance. The district of the Albaicín begins on the hill of the Chapiz, and from here there is a wide and lovely view of the city. At its foot stretches out the delightful part known as Cármenes which is a charming combination of small dwellings and orchards, and has the harmonious effect of lighting up the whole area with strokes of vivid colour.

This varied world—so individual and with such personality—is the heir to both the victors and the vanquished. It lies stretched out before our eyes, and in the distance, as the poet says:

*"Los dos ríos de Granada,
uno llanto y otro sangre."*

And the city lies at the gates of the Alhambra—its gallant and medieval heart.

THE SACROMONTE

Turning to the right off the old road to Guadix, from the Casa del Chapiz, one comes to Sacromonte, which is bounded on the left by the walls of the Alhambra.

As you climb up towards the mountain the road is bordered by cactus and prickly pears.

And suddenly the caves appear, deep inside the mountain, and the motley world of the gypsies lies before you.

These caves are whitewashed inside and out, and their walls are covered all over with pieces of local pottery, copper pots and multicoloured pictures. The sight of this local culture is most dramatic.

The notes of the guitar and the rhythmic clicking of the castanets make the background for hand claps which spur on the gypsy dancers.

*Inside the caves of the Sacromonte.
The bold dancing, the passionate songs,
the rhythm of the castenets and the
strumming of the guitar — at times
plaintive and at times full of fire —
reflect the unquenchable spirit of the
gypsies.*

HOLY WEEK

The religious festivals of Corpus Christi—which the Catholic Monarchs declared should be the official festival of Granada—and of Holy Week are celebrated with great pomp and splendour amd combine both solemnity and spontaneity. Many Brotherhoods file through the streets carrying beautiful statues on floats, some of which have great artistic value, having been carved by sculptors of the category of Martínez Montañés, José de Mora or Pedro de Mena, and add a cheerful gaiety to the otherwise serious occasion of Holy Week. The devotion of the people fills the air with deep religious feeling, and this overflows with fervour until it creates a never-to-be-forgotten spectacle of colour on the day of the famous procession of the gypsies.

On Good Friday the concentration of the faithful in the Campo del Príncipe is most impressive, and the same can be said of the start of the procession of the Virgen de las Angustias, the Patron Saint of Granada.

The Good Friday procession reaches the point of greatest enthusiasm as it arrives at the Campo del Príncipe, framed with green trees.

The statue of Cristo de los Gitanos (the Christ of the Gypsies) arouses great excitement as it passes through the streets of Granada in the celebrations of Holy Week.

*The revered
statue of Nuestra
Señora de las
Angustias
passing through
the Puerta de la
Justicia in the
Alhambra.
The perfect
combination of
art and religion
seems to surround
it with a halo.*

The Sacromonte omelette is a persuasive argument in favour of the cooking of Granada.

Two well known delicious sweets are "Huesos de Santo" and "Barretas".

THE COOKING OF GRANADA

It is a quirk of irony that underneath the restrained character of the people of Granada lies a hidden vein of eastern sensuousness and this manifests itself in many ways. Thus it is that the cooking of Granada has retained the traditional elements of Moorish Andalusia in which are combined two original gastronomic sources, the Moorish and the Christian.

Varied and appetizing are the typical dishes that the cooking of Granada offer to the palate of the gourmet. Among the best are the ham from Trevélez — cured in the cool air of the highest village in Spain and fried with the delicious beans from the plains of Granada; the noble omelette cooked in the Sacromonte manner; sardines in the Granada style; the exquisite almond soup of the simple and basic broth made from wheat — and as an aperitif a few morsels of ham from Trevélez taken with a glass of fine wine from Huéscar, Huétor or Albandón.

As to sweets, Granada has the most delicious and original varieties from the "Huesos de Santo" and the "Barretas" to the "Empanadillas de Santa Catalina", and also the "Tarta Real" from Motril — of Moorish origin — the "Huevos Moles" of San Antón, the "Batatines" of San Bernado or the "Polvorones" of the Clarisas de Chauchina. And there still remain many other excellent dishes too numerous to mention, such as the delightful "Borrachuelos", "Nochegüenos", "Voladillos" and "Felipes".

Truly for desserts Granada is the capital of Arab-Andalusian cookery.

THE SIERRA NEVADA

The great ridges of the Sierra Nevada, frosted with snow, raise their aristocratic outlines in the distance.

This mountain seems like a Titan grown old in the guardianship of the city, or perhaps it would be better to describe it as a timid but watchful lover consumed with perpetual anxiety.

The Sierra Nevada has always been the mythical back-drop against which appears the elegant city of Granada.

Some views of the white mountains of Granada, including a ski-lift and the Parador de Turismo in the Sierra Nevada.

On the Veleta
— the Virgin
of the Snows.

The poetic peaks of the Sierra Nevada have great majesty.

A statue of "Nuestra Señora de las Angustias", Patron Saint of Granada.

Contents

That ancient part of history which is Spain is often referred to as "the bull's skin", because that is the shape of Spain on the map. The aim of this book is to present a detailed and comprehensive picture of a fragment of that "bull's skin", and to help this it includes a number of spectacular photographs. The Editor will be well satisfied if he has succeeded in giving you a deeper and better knowledge of Spain.

Collection ALL EUROPE

Languages: Spanish, French, English, German, Italian, Catalan, Dutch, Swedish, Portuguese, Japanese, Arab

1 ANDORRA
2 LISBON
3 LONDON
4 BRUGES
5 PARIS
6 MONACO
7 VIENNA
8 NICE
9 CANNES
10 ROUSSILLON
11 VERDUN
12 THE TOWER OF LONDON
13 ANTWERP
14 WESTMINSTER ABBEY
15 THE SPANISH RIDING SCHOOL IN VIENNA
16 FATIMA
17 WINDSOR CASTLE
18 THE OPAL COAST
19 COTE D'AZUR
20 AUSTRIA
21 LOURDES
22 BRUSSELS

Collection ALL AMERICA

1 PUERTO RICO
2 SANTO DOMINGO

Collection ALL AFRICA

1 MOROCCO

Collection ART IN SPAIN

1 PALAU DE LA MUSICA CATALANA
(Catalan Palace of Music)
2 GAUDI
3 PRADO MUSEUM I (Spanish Painting)
4 PRADO MUSEUM II (Foreign Painting)
5 THE ROOF-BOSSES OF THE CATHEDRAL
OF GERONA
6 THE CASTLE OF XAVIER
7 THE ROMANESQUE STYLE IN SPAIN
8 SPANISH CASTLES
9 THE CATHEDRALS OF SPAIN
10 THE CATHEDRAL OF GERONA
11 GRAN TEATRO DEL LICEO DE BARCELONA
(The Great Opera House)
12 THE ROMANESQUE STYLE IN CATALONIA
13 LA RIOJA: ART TREASURES AND WINE-GROWING
RESOURCES
14 PICASSO
15 THE BAROQUE STYLE IN SPAIN
16 ROMAN REMAINS IN SPAIN
17 THE GOTHIC STYLE IN SPAIN
18 THE WINES OF CATALONIA
19 THE ALHAMBRA AND THE GENERALIFE
20 GRANADA AND THE ALHAMBRA (ARAB
AND MAURESQUE MONUMENTS OF CORDOVA,
SEVILLE AND GRANADA)

Collection ALL SPAIN

Languages: Spanish, French, English, German, Italian, Catalan, Dutch, Swedish, Portuguese, Japanese, Arab

1 ALL MADRID
2 ALL BARCELONA
3 ALL SEVILLE
4 ALL MAJORCA
5 ALL THE COSTA BRAVA
6 ALL MALAGA and the Costa del Sol
7 ALL THE CANARY ISLANDS I,
Lanzarote and Fuerteventura
8 ALL CORDOBA
9 ALL GRANADA
10 ALL VALENCIA
11 ALL TOLEDO
12 ALL SANTIAGO and the Rías Bajas
13 ALL IBIZA and Formentera
14 ALL CADIZ and the Costa de la Luz
15 ALL MONTSERRAT
16 ALL SANTANDER and the Costa Esmeralda
17 ALL THE CANARY ISLANDS II,
Tenerife, La Palma, Gomera, Hierro
18 ALL PEÑISCOLA
19 ALL SITGES
20 ALL BURGOS,
Covarrubias and Santo Domingo de Silos
21 ALL ALICANTE and the Costa Blanca
22 ALL NAVARRA
23 ALL LERIDA Province and Pyrenees
24 ALL SEGOVIA and Province
25 ALL SARAGOSSA and Province
26 ALL SALAMANCA and Province
27 ALL AVILA and Province
28 ALL MINORCA
29 ALL SAN SEBASTIAN and Province
30 ALL ASTURIAS
31 ALL CORUNNA and the Rías Altas
32 ALL TARRAGONA and Province
33 ALL MURCIA and Province
34 ALL VALLADOLID and Province
35 ALL GIRONA and Province
36 ALL HUESCA and Province
37 ALL JAEN and Province
38 ALL ALMERIA and Province
39 ALL CASTELLON and the Costa del Azahar
40 ALL CUENCA and Province
41 ALL LEON and Province
42 ALL PONTEVEDRA, VIGO and the Rías Bajas
43 ALL RONDA
44 ALL SORIA

The printing of this book was completed in the workshops of FISA - Industrias Gráficas, Palaudarias, 26 - Barcelona (Spain)